A true happy place is a place deep inside
that bubbles and glistens and glows.

It grows from the seeds that we plant in the world
when love and our gratitude flows.

In our happy place we will treasure all life
and love and embrace who we are.

We'll nourish our minds and nurture our souls
and radiate light like a star.

- Helene Pam

ISBN 13: 978-0692792285
10: 0692792287

How to use this journal

Get creative and have fun drawing, writing, pasting, coloring, and experiencing the many exercises and activites in your Happy Place journal. These will help deepen your insight into who you are, as well as build confidence, good relationships, and an awareness of the important role you play in the lives of others and the world.

Self-Reflection
1

School and Hobbies
2

Family and Friends
3

Helping the World
4

Note for your grown up

The exercises in this journal were developed based on well-researched techniques of personal growth and happiness.

The Four Sections of the Journal

This is me!!!

Draw or paste a picture of yourself.

SELF - REFLECTION

The beauty that comes from
within shines the brightest.

Watch your tree grow
throughout this journal.

Color me in.
Reflect on your
inner beauty.

Things I love best about ME

(Write, draw, or paste in each frame.)

No human on earth came from the same mould...

Things that make me SMILE

(Write, draw, or paste in each frame.)

Helpful tip: If there is something that you don't understand, you can always ask a grown up.

...but each has a purpose to find and unfold.

BIG DREAMS

The
dreams
that
make
us
WHOLE
are embedded in our SOUL.

A wish is a reflection of our HEART'S desire.

On each **cloud** write or draw your dreams. On each **star** write or draw your wishes.

Little Wishes

Gratitude waters our soul and cultivates our happiness.

MY
GRATITUDE
TREE

There is always something to be grateful for.

On each **leaf** write or draw something that you are grateful for.

Free Space!!!

Express yourself!

SCHOOL AND HOBBIES

Knowledge opens hidden
windows to the world.

Color me in.
It is exercise for
your brain.

- School -

Achievements

Write or draw the things
that made you proud.

GREAT JOB!

Lessons learnt are the unspoken
achievements that change lives.

- Hobby -

Achievements

Write or draw the things that made you proud.

You were born with special gifts that only you can bring into the world.

YOU ROCK!

GET MOVING
Get Your Heart Pumping

Your Pick!

- ☐ Run
- ☐ Dance
- ☐ Jump
- ☐ Cycle
- ☐ Do Sports
- ☐ _____

IT FEELS GREAT

Make time to move for at least 20 minutes, 3 times a week. It helps your mind, body, and spirit.

Things I want to learn:

Hobbies I want to try:

There are no *limits* to what you *can* ACHIEVE.

SCHOOL GOALS

High

Aim

Set

Goals

On each **flower** write a goal and steps to achieve it.

HOBBY GOALS

Work

Hard

Never

Quit

GOALS
ARE
PLANS
THAT
MAKE
DREAMS
COME
TRUE.

Free Space!!!

Have fun!

FAMILY AND FRIENDS

Love is a language that needs
no words yet we all understand.

Color me in.
It will help you to
focus and feel calm.

People I love

& who love me

Write, draw, or paste photos of your loved ones.

True
LOVE
has ♥ no
boundaries.

HUG A LOVED ONE

How does it make you feel?

& SAY "I LOVE YOU"

REMINDER:

Give a hug every day.

How can I help out more at home?

MAKE HOME YOUR HAPPY PLACE!

Deeds of love affirm the words 'I love you'.

How can I be a better friend?

GOOD FRIENDSHIPS = HAPPINESS

Write or draw letters to your loved ones.

Thanks

Feelings of love should never be left unspoken.

Joy

Love

Share these letters
with them.

Free Space!!!

Make it yours!

HELPING THE WORLD

Turning compassion into action
will make your heart smile.

Color me in.
Relax and
contemplate.

WAYS I CAN HELP MY COMMUNITY

Ideas to get started:

Greet everyone with a smile.

Be a friend to someone who needs one.

Donate your unwanted toys to children in need.

Thank someone who has helped your community.

Collect canned goods for a food bank.

Visit a senior center.

Thank You!

Plant seeds of love and grow fields of happiness.

ACTIVITY TIME

Pick a day
SMILE AT EVERYONE

Draw or paste a picture of your smile.

How many people smiled back? #

Did you feel the magic of smiling?

A smile spreads rays of sunshine.

What I love about
our Earth

Nature is a kaleidoscope of beauty on a moving canvas.

SPEND TIME IN NATURE

Use your senses:

>LOOK
>SMELL
>LISTEN
>FEEL

Draw or describe
your experience.

WAYS THAT I CAN HELP TAKE CARE OF OUR EARTH

Conserve Water

Recycle and Compost

Eat Less Animal Products

Walk More, Drive Less

Plant More Trees

Add a check when you make progress.

MORE IDEAS TO HELP TAKE CARE OF OUR EARTH

If you want a world of light, we each have to shine.

POW

BE AWESOME

BE A HERO

Well done on completing your journal.

We are so happy that we could help guide you through this journey.

We would love to hear from you. Please connect with us on our Website, Facebook, or Twitter to share your stories, experiences, and photos, and to find many free activities.

If you loved this journal, please take a moment to review it on Amazon to help spread happiness and inspiration.

Helene & Sheleen
(Mom-Daughter Team)

 www.PurpleSplashStudios.com

 Facebook.com/PurpleSplashStudios

 Twitter.com/PurpleSplashS

Through inner reflection you've planted new seeds,
and now understand what true healthy growth needs.

You know that real beauty comes from a deep place,
and life holds more meaning than winning a race.

Our world is connected; that's something we share,
and love and compassion can spread everywhere.

You're born with a purpose and not to fill space.
So shine and spread light from your bright happy place.

- Helene Pam

Spread
your
wings

and allow your
DREAMS
to
s o a r.

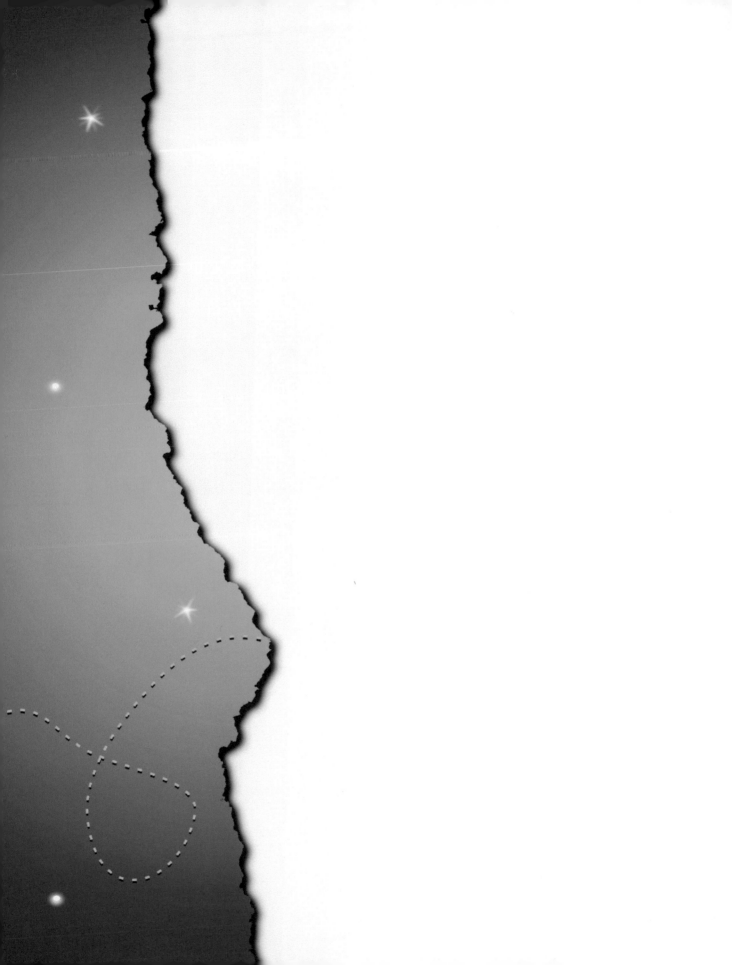

Made in the USA
Lexington, KY
04 November 2016